T0381025

A Mother's Journey

by Allison
King-Ramsey

Illustrated by
Noah I Ramsey

AuthorHouse™
1663 Liberty Drive
Bloomington, IN 47403
www.authorhouse.com
Phone: 833-262-8899

This book is printed on acid-free paper.

ISBN: 978-1-7283-7735-3 (sc)
ISBN: 978-1-7283-7736-0 (hc)
ISBN: 978-1-7283-7737-7 (e)

Library of Congress Control Number: 2023900670

Print information available on the last page.

Published by AuthorHouse 01/18/2023

authorHOUSE

A Mother's Journey

A Mother I set
out not to be...

I wanted more out of **LIFE** …
you see….

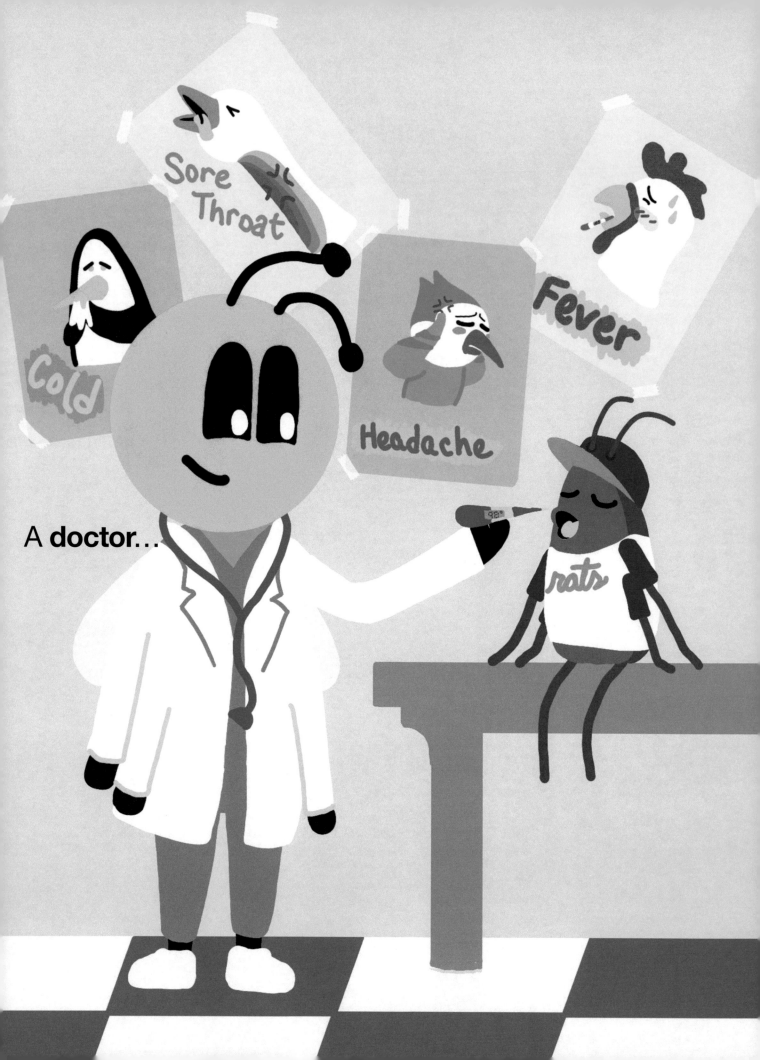

A **doctor**…

A lawyer....

Anything else will do….

It really wasn't my **reality...**

I strive for **more** not less…
you see.

Then I became a **Mom...**

What kind of **Mom** would I be?

Oh the JOY…
the STRESS…
the LOVE…
just for ME!

I then realized this was my **REALITY!**

My goal...
I set out from the first day...

I wanted to give more than I could ever receive.

My children would have a mom that CARES...

Their **PAIN...**

A Mom that creates a home of **PEACE** and **LOVE**…

As close to the one in **HEAVEN** above.

As we learn together to LOVE GOD's WAY!

Today the world knows how much you mean to me.

But what's more **important,**

Is what they don't **see!**

Oh the **PAIN!**

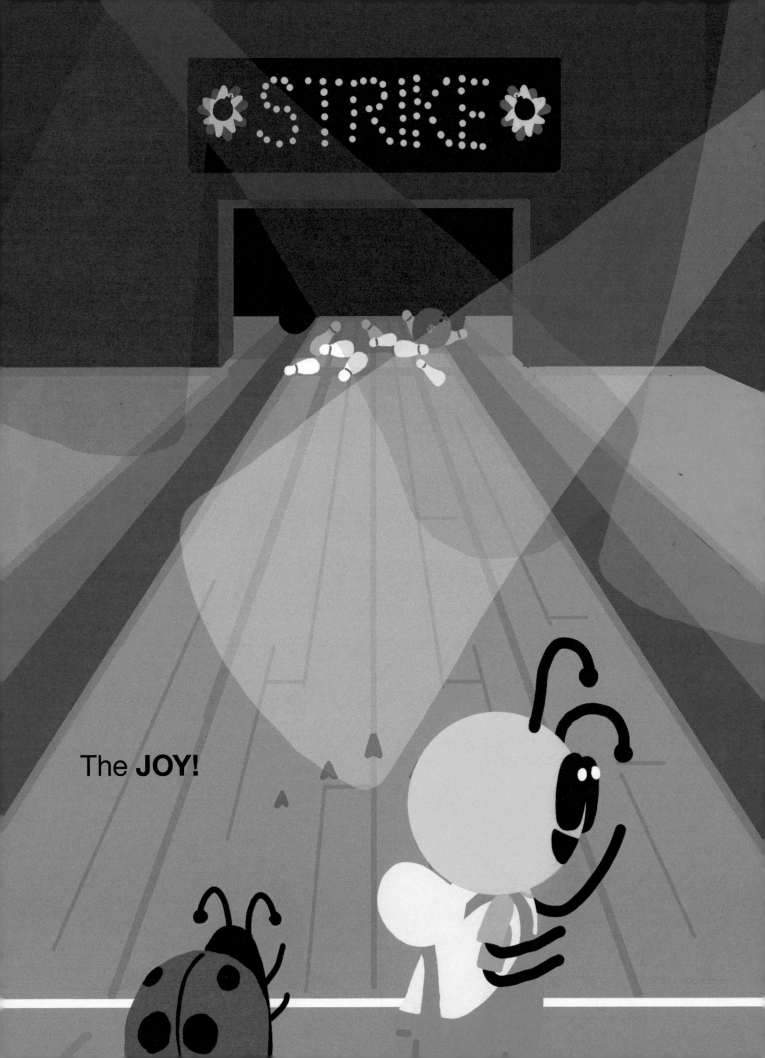

The **JOY!**

Just for **ME!**

As I remember…

A MOM...

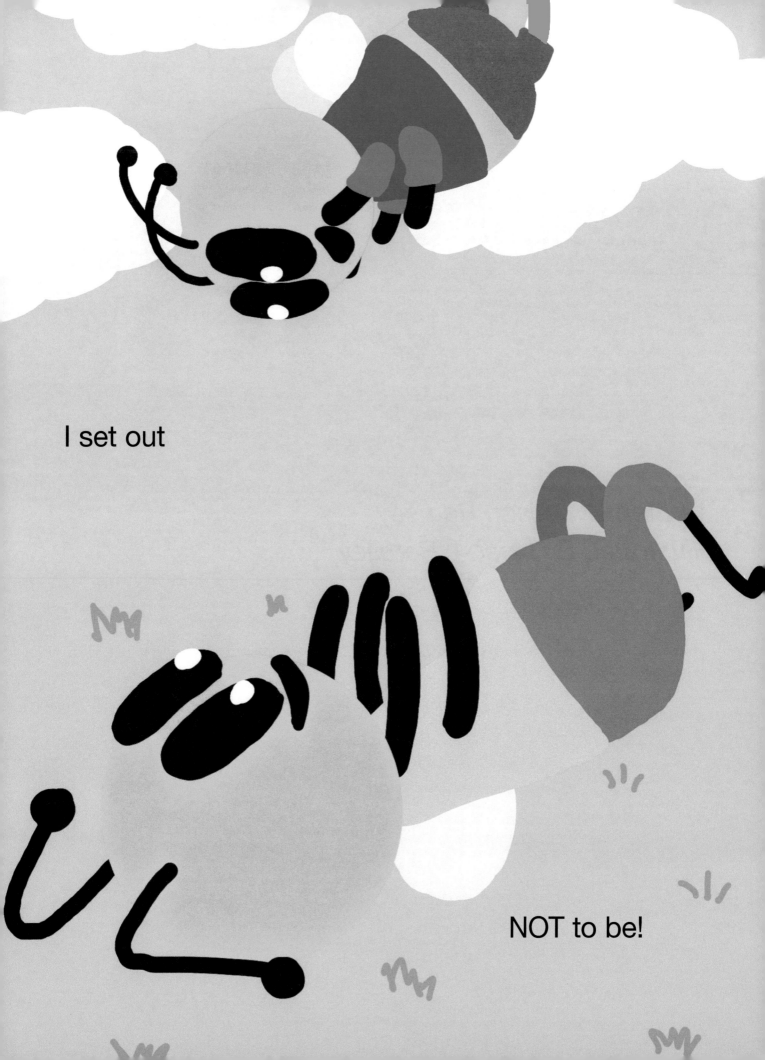

I set out

NOT to be!

Written By Allison Ramsey
Illustrated By Noah I. Ramsey

About the Author

An educator in the Metro Atlanta area for over 25 years. The love of reading with the combination of adding to a child's self-worth has inspired her to write this book. She is married with two children and two grandchildren.

Printed in the United States
by Baker & Taylor Publisher Services